The Prince

A Bluffer's Handbook

to

Machiavelli's *The Prince*

GILGAMESH BOOKS

RECLAIMED CLASSICS

Cover image:
Portrait of Niccolò di Bernardo dei Machiavelli
by Santi di Tito
(1469)

THE PRINCE

- A Bluffer's Handbook to Machiavelli's The Prince -

The Prince needs little introduction but it can benefit greatly by an extended elucidation. The influence of the work has extended far beyond its modest pages and its subsequent authority and deeper meaning can easily be missed, even by the most engaged reader. This '*ante* foreword' then, aims to cover as broadly as possible such details that will illuminate the reader and further their understanding of what is a divisive and yet instructive work.

Niccolò Machiavelli, whose father was a lawyer and brilliant tutor, was irreverent, witty, friendly, loyal to his friends, attracted to and by women and even wrote the best comedy of his day, the *Mandrake.* Little is known of his early life until we reach the end of the 15th century.

In 1494 Charles VIII of France crossed the Alps and invaded France. Florence erupted in the ensuing chaos and the then leader Piero the Unfortunate, Lorenzo de' Medici's son and successor, went to meet the French King. He surrendered unconditionally but when he returned to the city he was harangued as a traitor and forced into exile with his family. He had barely ruled for two years.

The vacuum was filled by the dynamic Dominican friar Girolamo Savonarola, who persuaded the king not to sack Florence. Savonarola was not qualified for political office due to the fact that he was a cleric and secondly because he was not a Florentine citizen. However, he made his influence felt at government level through the political group the *Frateschi*. Fra Girolamo was known for his prophecies, eulogies of social grandeur and calls for a Christian revival. He denounced priestly corruption, oppressive rule and the exploitation of the poor. His government ushered in democratic reforms and permitted many exiles to return home. Despite the strident advances in secular legislation and law, Savonarola's true motive was to create a 'city of god'. Citizens threw off showy garments, and numerous women joined religious orders. Above all, Savonarola came to be remembered for organising the '*Bonfire of the Vanities*', where he consigned all 'vanities', such as perfume, paintings, wigs and even ancient manuscripts, to the flames.

Savonarola's Florence collapsed within a year, and the Dominican father was summoned to Rome after having accused Pope Alexander VI of corruption. He refused to attend and was excommunicated and banned from speaking in public. Florence had also challenged independent Pisa and the short-lived war was an unmitigated disaster, which caused severe food shortages. There were even cases of the plague and Savonarola was blamed for the catastrophe being visited upon them. The citizens once more instigated change and tired of the friar's religious rantings, Savonarola was arrested in 1498 and charged with heresy on spurious charges. Under torture he confessed that his visions were false and he was burnt at the stake in Florence's beautiful Piazza della Signoria, along with two lieutenants. A nascent Golden Age of democracy had therefore been extinguished in the impure flames of inquisitional Italy.

Piero Soderini was elected as president for life and the republic flourished during a brief period marked by the absence of fraud and a continuance of democracy. Niccolò Machiavelli was instated as the secretary to the Second Chancery of the *Signoria*, known as *i dieci*, the ten. He was not eligible to be an ambassador as he was not of noble birth. He was also the Secretary for War and led a successful campaign against Pisa. He also prompted the use of a citizen's militia thus removing dependence on erratic mercenary forces. Now began the politician's inroads into international affairs and power games. He was sent to papal elections and met Pope Alexander VI, who he considered a master of political deception. He also appeared before King Luis XII of France and Maximilian the Holy Roman Emperor, both of whom Machiavelli thought very little. In fact, the only leader that he did have some admiration for was Cesare Borgia, Pope Alexander VI's son. Cesare Borgia, known as the Duke of Valentinois (*Duca Valentino*, in Italian), was considered by Machiavelli to be a role model prince. He was a leader who exercised his power well and would have united all of Italy had fate not intervened and illness put an early end to his life. And while being a legend in his own time he was also ruthless, depraved, and wielded violence in the best of Machiavellian manners, which was in the aid of a lucid political goal. Leaders were invited to peace talks and then assassinated in textbook Agathocles-style.

In September 1512 Soderini was repudiated when Cardinal Giovanni de Medici captured Florence with Papal troops during the War of the League of Cambrai and the citizen militia was crushed by battle hardened Spanish troops. This restored the Medici rule of Florence and with the return of one of Europe's most notable families and Pope Leo X ruling as proxy from Rome, Machiavelli was arrested, charged with conspiring against the Medici and then tortured. He was finally released in an amnesty by the Pope and then exiled to his family estate south of the city limits.

Machiavelli had had *ex officio* control of the military and ambassadors while also acting as envoy and diplomat. Now he found himself a bored and hard up land holder. In frustration at the loss of purpose to his life he took pen to paper and began writing his discourses on Republican government, only to abandon them almost at once and write out his most famous work in just three months. In so doing he completed what has been deemed the most famous job application letter in history. It was a document that, in its essence, offered a blueprint for how to maintain power in the face of undermining forces.

Machiavelli finished *The Prince* in order to make a favourable impression on a would-be Medici patron. Machiavelli asked his friend '*the Magnificent Francesco Vettori, His Patron and Benefactor, Florentine Ambassador to the Supreme Pontiff. In Rome*' to pass it on to the Medici. Here is part of the accompanying letter he wrote explaining his reasons for presenting such a work to Vettori:

'I am unashamed to converse with them [local villagers] and to question them about the motives for their actions, and they, out of their human kindness, answer me. And for four hours at a time I feel no boredom, I forget all my troubles, I do not dread poverty, and I am not terrified by death. I absorb myself into them completely. And because Dante says that no one understands anything unless he retains what he has understood, I have jotted down what I have profited from in their conversation and composed a short study, De principatibus, in which I delve as deeply as I can into the ideas concerning this topic, discussing the definition of a princedom, the categories of princedoms, how they are acquired, how they are retained, and why they are lost. And if ever any whimsy of mine has given you pleasure, this one should not displease you. It ought to be welcomed by a prince, and especially by a new prince; therefore I am dedicating it to His Magnificence Giuliano.'

He continues:

'I am wasting away and cannot continue on like this much longer without becoming contemptible because of my poverty. Besides, there is my desire that these Medici princes should

begin to engage my services, even if they should start out by having me roll along a stone.'

The work was dedicated to Lorenzo di Piero de' Medici, grandson of 'Lorenzo the Magnificent'. Lorenzo was part of the family that ruled Florence and his uncle, Giovanni, was Pope Leo X at the time. As a book it was never published in his lifetime and although a Medici did receive a copy, the recipient never gave any indication that he had read it.

Machiavelli also wrote it at a time in human history when Copernicus was studying the heavens and Leonardo anatomised the machinery of Mother Nature. In this fashion Niccolò dissected the inner workings of man the political animal. He wanted to understand the secrets of state craft as had been understood in ancient Rome by such great men as Tacitus and Seneca.

The book's subject matter was organised along the lines of new princedoms; mixed princedoms; totally new states; defense and military; the qualities of a prince and finally the prudence of the prince.

In writing of new princedoms he referred to all forms of organized government as the 'state', whether they were princely or republican. He believed hereditary princedoms were less trouble to rule '*unless extraordinary vices cause him to be hated, it is reasonable to expect that his subjects will be naturally well disposed towards him*'. He also made his motives for his work clear by stating that he was writing for new rulers.

When tackling the topic of mixed princedoms he made the distinction between new conquests of long-established states that were annexed, the conquering of centrally governed kingdoms and ordered states that had clearly defined laws. Firstly, he offered advice on how to hold a recently acquired territory by using the Roman republic as an example. You could colonise the land, curry favour with the existing power structure while simultaneously curtailing its limits or alternatively crush their influence, which was how William the Conqueror initially subdued England when he wiped out almost the entire English nobility in just one afternoon, thereby creating a governing vacuum. He went on to emphasis the need for planning ahead and to beware of the winds of fortune blowing against you.

Where the King was a central ruler then such a hierarchy was difficult to take over, but once the blood-line had been dismissed the land was easy to maintain. The famous example that Machiavelli used to illustrate his point was Alexander the Great dethroning

Darius III and thereby conquering the Persian Empire. He advised the planting of colonies and the ruler taking root in the territory or alternatively setting up a puppet regime but leaving local customs in place.

As for the creation of totally new states, virtue and fortune had much to do with long-term success. A prince that achieved rule through his own ability would find the rise to power fraught with tribulations but once he had consolidated his position, he would find it relatively much easier to maintain such control. This was because such a self-supporting personality would have dealt with his enemies on the road to power and would have gained a wherewithal while navigating a route through the hallways of power. Machiavelli did, however, warn the new prince that provoking change was the most dangerous act for a new ruler as people were naturally adverse to significant political transformation.

Contrary to the prince who took the seat of power through his own initiatives, the prince who was aided and abetted would find his ascension relatively free of obstacles but once emplaced he would discover that his had become dependent upon his backers, who also controlled the army and the factions that preserved order in the realm. Here Machiavelli cited Cesare

Borgia as the exception that broke the rule. He was assisted by his father Pope Alexander VI but while given a foot up, he also possessed the same capabilities that any self-made prince instinctively had. He not only secured his power base but also greatly extended it. His rule was, however, dependent on mercenary armies loyal to the Orsini brothers and the support of the French king.

If a prince planned to commit murder or a grave act of wrongdoing to wrest control from opponents, then it had to be carefully calculated beforehand. This was referred to as '*criminal virtue*'. The evil deed had to be executed in a single blow and then the new prince had to follow the rest of his reign with contrary behavior. This allowed the populace to forget previous digressions, such as the putting to death of political rivals, and more importantly for the ruler to regain his reputation, which though briefly lost was not irreparably so.

Machiavelli now offered an alternative route to power and that was through the popular support of the people. This path would ensure that the prince could control the powerful, whereas the previous examples, where the would-be ruler was supported by the powerful, only guaranteed the control of the people.

Here the writer made use of Agathocles of Syracuse to illustrate his argument. The Sicilian magnate utterly decimated the established oligarchy, thereby gaining immediate control but he did not attain the blessing of the people. Machiavelli advised the prince that he should make sure that the people needed him, especially when there was a crisis and he would be required to be equal to the circumstance.

The author ended this section by discussing how best to judge the strength of a principality based on its ability to defend itself and the extent to which it depended on its allies. He then analysed the church as if it were a princedom, drawing special attention to its successes and ultimate weakness due to its theological factions.

The next subject for educating a prince was the central theme of defense and the military. The two load-bearing pillars of state were sound laws and effective military force. Mercenary armies were to be avoided at all cost and a citizen army to be raised in its place. This Machiavelli argued from experience as he had acted upon this knowledge when he was Minister for War for the Florentine Republic and he carried this notion forcefully into his teachings.

The following five chapters now dealt with the qualities of a prince, covering a range of virtues or vices. While the book structure adhered to the vogue of *mirrors for princes* style, which offered customary counsel for rulers, the suggestions turned out to be anything but conventional and it is here that *The Prince* has earned its infamy in world literature. What the unexpectant reader would digest may have alarmed and even enlightened but it has rarely left anyone indifferent.

A Prince's primary duty was to understand military matters as *'being disarmed makes you despised.'* By taking war seriously he not only earned the respect of his soldiers, upon which his power ultimately rested but he also secured his realm from attack. Today we all see images of members of royal families the world over doing their military service. There is also the oft repeated history of the left being taken over by a right-wing dictatorship as the left has always been unsuccessful in securing the army's allegiance, the death of Allende is a case in point. Maybe Machiavelli had a legitimate point here. Before offering a social revolution and intellectual salvation for the people, first get the army on board. Hugo Chávez understood this and was a military man first; a social revolutionary second. He secured the army's loyalty before he embarked on trying to restructure society from the top down. Eventually, this saved his life during the right-wing coup d'état. He is also the exception that proves the rule.

Not all positive attributes were necessarily good in a leader and vice-versa when it came to negative traits. It was impossible to have all the qualities that a good leader should possess. However, Machiavelli offered light at the end of the tunnel for the personality-impaired prince. He should not over concern himself in this aspect. Those points of character or virtues that he did not hold he should only give the illusion that he was virtuous, even if he occasionally went against such high-brow principals. He should naturally avoid any evil acts but if the moment required cruelty then me must not shy from it either. Here we have the leader as actor. He had to aspire to greatness even if he did not fulfill its basic requirements. We need look no further than our own experience of political rhetoric and subsequent bombing campaigns by some western leaders in the interests of 'freedom and democracy' to confirm Machiavelli's premise. This was almost Orwellian *Doublethink* where two contradictory ideas could be held by a thinker while believing both of them. Here though, it was more important for the electorate to believe this than for the politician to do so. So a leader's actions could be unsaintly but he should nonetheless be able to discern between right and wrong. In modern democratic times, if the leader runs astray then we at least have parliament to unseat him (or now her) from their cabinet.

Machiavelli analyses in quick succession the pros and cons of generosity as against parsimony; cruelty when pitted against mercy; when a prince should keep his word and finally how best he could avoid contempt and hatred. Machiavelli importantly pointed out that '*Men worry less about doing an injury to one who makes himself loved than to one who makes himself feared.*' Hence '*it is better to be feared than loved*'; which was the book's most infamous aphorism. The author compares the leadership of two historic rival generals: Hannibal and Scipio Africanus. Hannibal maintained order in the ranks of his disparate soldiers through fear. This was his '*inhuman cruelty*', which was seen as a virtue. Scipio meanwhile suffered mutiny twice and frequent dissension because he was lenient and therefore showed '*excessive mercy*', which encouraged his soldiers to be bold and challenge his authority.

The author closed this section by saying that it was important for a leader to keep his word and when he was compromised by it then he should at least give the 'illusion' that he was consistent in what he promised. Going against one's word should therefore only occur in cases of extreme want. He also went on to reiterate the case of men being contented when their property rights were not infringed and their women were let be, *'A man sooner forgets the death of a father than the loss of their inheritance.'* Christianity in part came to the fore because it offered lesser men protection of their womenfolk from meddling superiors. Under God's divine law, marriage was sacrosanct. By respecting these basic rights of his subjects a prince could significantly evade the contempt of those he chose to rule.

The last group of themes that Machiavelli ended with, concerned the prudence of a prince and he said, *'A prince needs to have the discernment to recognize the good or bad in what another says or does even though he has no acumen himself'*. The emplacement of fortresses in conquered territories did not always have the desired effect and conversely was unsuccessful. Such a measure provoked the ire of the affected people and this Machiavelli had already told the prince to avoid. Even today after Edward I's great castle building scheme and forced colonisation of English settlers in Wales, established as they were at the base of each of the fortified outposts, the Welsh are far from subsumed by the wider nation of England. The boarder of where northern and southern England begins and ends is lost in time and the two regions are welded together by the Midlands. However, Wales is clearly joined at the hip and has never been a comfortable addition to the English body politic, despite the gesture of the crown prince carrying the nation's name.

Honour can be obtained through derring-do and Machiavelli offered succinct advice to princes caught in a conflict. The author insisted that it was indispensable to take a side in any dispute, rather than remain impartial, but there were conditions to such involvement. You could always profit from your ally's successes and if you were the more powerful partner you stood to gain more than they would. Also, should your ally lose you would always have an ally.

Before signing off, Machiavelli outlined the reasons why the princes of Italy had lost their states, which was one of the motivating factors that prompted the young diplomat to lay out his ideas in the first place. He then brought his provocative work to a close by focusing on fortune and how one had to mould it by taking opportune risks, '*it is better to be impetuous than cautious, because fortune is a woman; and it is necessary, if one wants to hold her down, to beat her and strike her down.*' The disconcerting and well-quoted metaphor certainly illustrates that the book was written in different times to our own. He also used a less controversial and indeed clearer similitude by comparing fortune to a river in full flow. When the torrent was raging, risk would be the only course of action but while it was calm one could erect dams and levees thereby preparing for less predictable weather ahead and thus lessen its impact.

His last chapter told us much of what propelled him to pick up his pen and argue his thesis the way he did. Here he called upon the ruling Medici to seize Italy and thus free her from the '*barbarians*'. The Pope at the time of the book's composition was Leo X, a Medici, and this call to arms directly invoked the papal seat as a principal play maker in material politics.

Machiavelli mentioned throughout his work a diverse range of great men from history to exemplify the validity of his conclusions. Achilles is used to demonstrate that the classic writers showed it was necessary to merge the methods of both man and beast.

Achilles had been trained by Chiron the centaur and so the ultimate hero should be a combination between man's laws and a beast's brute strength.

Spain's King Fernando was mentioned recurrently as a ruler who had achieved greatness due to astute political scheming. He sermonized on harmony and devotion yet his actions clearly betrayed his words. Nonetheless, Machiavelli considered the king's apparent hypocrisy to be acceptable and even necessary.

The Roman Emperor Marcus Aurelius, who ruled in fair and modest measure, was the only successful ruler who did not side with the army. Machiavelli quoted him as an example of a righteous 'prince' with a consolidated power base.

Pope Julius II, who succeeded Pope Alexander, achieved wide ranging successes in the field of combat and in the political arena. He enhanced the influence of the Church, raised substantial funds through the sale of ecclesiastical offices, which impressed Machiavelli, and ultimately repelled the French with the intervention of the Holy League. Machiavelli believed that such sweeping accomplishment was the express result of a ruler's impulsive actions as opposed to an inactive head of state. This was a time when Popes had concubines and children and there were orgies in the Vatican.

Moses earned the highest of Machiavelli's accolades. The biblical leader was praised as having achieved control through his own aptitudes; fortune had not come to his aid. The case of Moses leading an enslaved people to freedom was the ideal parable for the bondage of Machiavelli's Italy perpetually trapped by foreign cupidity. It is here as he signs off that Machiavelli makes his plea for such a leader to guide his people and thus liberate them from the degenerate invaders.

So much then, for what the book tells us. The questions now are what does it teach us and what essential conclusions has history's impressionable readership drawn? Here opinions are fundamentally divided. Even simple definitions require clarification, not just for the modern reader but also for the late medieval mind. Machiavelli used unorthodox definitions for 'virtue' and 'prudence', which was in direct contrast to the existing religious meanings of the words. However, he was not out of sync in the wider tradition of European political thought where the terms had a far deeper and more ancient use by the Greco-

Romans. Machiavelli's usage of the terms signified glory hunting and strong-willed character and was aligned with the founding influences of European culture and history.

However, his novelty went much further than this in stirring up the world of humanistic thought. His distinct break with the past came through his open and public declaration of the concept of establishing a new state through the use of unjust measures and immoral actions. It abandoned a more reserved scholastic tradition that had been handed down to Machiavelli's generation, and starkly challenged the predominant political philosopher of Catholic Europe, namely Aristotle. The fact that Machiavelli continually referred to Xenophon more than Plato, Aristotle, and Cicero combined, said much of his break with the conventional political authorities. Xenophon's the *Education of Cyrus* was one of the classic 'mirrors of princes', which were texts offering advice to the ruling élite.

Machiavelli referred to the subject matter of his book as a simple summary of his knowledge on *'the actions of great men'*, drawn from his reading and more significantly his extensive personal experience. Although the writer approached his question with candour and unambiguous language, calling for realism instead of idealism, the advice given shocked even contemporaries, as it still does today. Therefore, its importance in political thought as a viable addition to the nature of human thought is still deeply questioned. And yet, the theory that obligation justified dishonourable actions was widely acknowledged by most thinkers of ancient civilisation.

In many ways Machiavelli pursued amoral realism and with it offered us nothing new except the common sense of politics as we already experience it. There was not even the revelation of any hidden internal workings of the political mind. It was, though, the first time that such cut-throat declarations had been put down in writing for common consumption, and with it this sincere disclosure accordingly enabled society to debate the merits of such humanly flawed actions.

Machiavelli's patent language and writing style, which deliberately avoided embellishment, would ensure better decisions were made as one would see things as they really were and not as one wished they were. This was the exact opposite of the teaching of Cervantes' *Don Quixote*. It has been argued that the real audience for the book was the common man as rulers well understood the techniques laid out in the text. It is certain that the layman had most to learn, but that all rulers were conscious of the book's teachings and were capable practitioners of its material is highly questionable.

Although Machiavelli mapped out new territory in political thinking, his feeling that Italy needed a reform in rule if it were ever to free itself from foreign intervention and ultimately attain some semblance of nationhood was in keeping with his time. Machiavelli focused on this absence of power at a time when there was no such coherent unifying entity. He grappled with the central questions of how to seize power and then more importantly how maintain to it. He drew his conclusions from the rulers about him and the teachings handed down to him from Rome and then pieced together a best fit treatise.

Accordingly, Machiavelli gave us a clear perspective of the persona of the political realist, '*A man who neglects what should be done from what is actually done is on the road to self destruction.*' Lincoln was a good example of Machiavellian leadership in a democracy, who was accused of being egocentric when he suspended *habeas corpus*, and for having stepped beyond the bounds of the Constitution. Machiavelli's modern Prince probably most resembled Lenin who made the poor rich and rich poor. Despite Lenin's similarity to the book's protagonist, Marxists saw a perfect comparison with Stalin, who was in many ways the personification of the '*end justifies the means*', which Machiavelli worded as, '*in the actions of all men and especially of princes where there is no court of appeal one judges by the result.*' However, this well-worn axiom is perchance summoned upon when the conditions do not merit such radical measures. They are restrictive controls which better serve interests invested in power and rarely the better interests of those which power was primarily derived to serve.

Machiavelli also furnished us with the political actor; a leader who would or would not keep his word but always had to appear to act on principal and avoid all suspicion of being calculating, *"Everyone sees what you appear to be, few experience what you really are."*

Often Machiavelli's writings appear paradoxical when fear can be useful but hatred is counterproductive. Vices can bring riches and virtues can bring calamity. A prince had to attain power and all methods were outwardly encouraged, but Machiavelli insisted that it had to be glorious power *Gloria duplicata,* literally 'Double glory', and, '*He should not deviate from what is good if that is possible but he should know how to do evil if that is necessary.'*

An important theme was *fortuna*, which was a metaphor for the capricious nature of good fortune. For that reason *The Prince* is considered by some as a book offering advice on how to get lucky, '*Fortune favours the brave*'. Cesare Borgia was successful at the outset but eventually succumbed to his enemies because he was taken seriously ill and thereby fell to misfortune. Hence, the capable leader should be able to follow the winds of fortune, judging when best to be clement and when it was more expedient to be cruel. Borgia's fate was merely an extreme case of how the unforeseen could end a successful reign abruptly.

A prominent allegory regularly quoted from Machiavelli's pages was that of the lion and the fox, which was more than likely taken from the writings of Cicero. The Prince, Machiavelli tells us, had to acquire the guile of the fox to sense the trap that awaited him and the fortitude of the lion to fight off conspirators.

His provocative rhetoric made readers sit up and take note. Any form of political thought had to henceforth include a lucid denunciation of Machiavelli's assumptions if it wished to stand on its own as a legitimate hypothesis. Love or loathe Machiavelli's book for making evident a series of alarming maxims, he cannot be ignored. If your end is the preservation of your state and its people then you must be willing to do all in your power to attain those goals. Whether this is deemed tolerable plainly depended on the critic's interpretation of consequential ethics.

It has even been argued that Machiavelli wrote his dialectic as a satire and this was surprisingly the standard reading of the work during the 18th century by the Enlightenment *philosophes*. Great thinkers such as Diderot and Jean-Jacques Rousseau adhered to this interpretation. Therefore, according to this analysis, *The Prince* was in actual fact a deliberate attempt to emphasize the advantages of open republics over restrictive monarchies. It was a trap for a prince to fall into and by following Machiavelli's sound steps he would inadvertently pave the way for a stable republic. However, so the theory states, Lorenzo de' Medici did not trust the author and the status quo continued unaltered. The reader should decide if this was the clandestine master plan or not.

Even if we reject every conclusion made in the book, the work has at least set down in one modest and clearly written text a political model that is objectionable on many levels. If we know what we do not agree with, then the work has defined those things that we do value. But what is the modest and clearly written text offering a political model that we do find palatable? Capitalism has no such guide book for how to maintain power and appease the masses, so are we back to square one with *The Prince*? Of course not, we must not forget Aristotle's *Republic*, the writings of Tacitus, Cicero and Seneca that have already been mentioned as alternatives to Machiavelli but also criticised by him for not getting to the point. So far then, Machiavelli has no equivalent plainly written adversary.

The Florentine's literary legacy has seen his fortunes rise and fall. Now his scholastic redemption is coming about due to a new interpretation of his writing. One striking fact about Machiavelli that is now evident, but was previously overlooked, is how *un*-Machiavellian he really was. As opposed to encouraging cruelty he actually told us not to be malicious or we would be hated and never told us that cruelty and treachery were virtues, *'His behaviour must be tempered by humanity and prudence, so that excessive distrust does not make him unbearable.'*

Neither was his own political career *Machiavellian*. He was not renowned for deceitful acts and did not employ fraudulent methods in order to keep his office once the Medici returned to power. He could have betrayed the Republic to his own advantage when he was arrested but he did not. Had he gone over to the Medici from the start or not been arrested, it is quite likely that the *The Prince* and subsequent publications would not have been produced. He was therefore more a statesman than plotter; more thinker than conniver. His ascendency and decline was of his own making and not at the cost of another.

'There should be no doubt about my word; for, since I have always kept it, I should not start learning how to break it now. Whoever has been honest and faithful for forty-three years, as I have, is unable to change his nature; my poverty is a witness to my loyalty and honesty.'

Machiavelli

The reason why *The Prince* continues in print and furnishes the bookshelves of political science undergraduates is due to its irrepressible influence. Although it was not the first book to offer a ruler advice about power, it has become the most notorious due to its profound effect on western political theory and practical application in real politics.

Apparently England's Henry VIII found pointers in the work to assist his protestant reforms and theologically opposed Spain's Catholic Charles V also kept a copy. Even England's Thomas Cromwell thought highly of the work and as Lord Protector he became the nation's dictator. The Protestants condemned it as a Catholic work while the Catholics damned it as a Protestant book. For these reasons *The Prince* has been referred to as the '*Koran of the courtiers*.'

His discourse on the accruement of power became an accepted premise for 17th century European political dialogue of the Catholic Counter Reformation. While Machiavelli was disparaged by prominent writers of the movement they also followed some of the Florentine scribe's fundamental pronouncements. However, they regarded Tacitus as a superior political realist.

British and French writers, especially, across the centuries were also persuaded by the *The Prince*; writers such as Bodin, Francis Bacon, John Milton, Rousseau, Hume, Edward Gibbon, and Adam Smith. Even the great philosophers, such as Descartes, Hobbes, Locke, Montaigne, and Montesquieu are thought to have reflected the peculiar political vision of Machiavelli in some of their musings.

From the thinkers to modern men of action, Napoleon wrote about *The Prince* and the comments were discovered in his carriage when he was captured after Waterloo. Mussolini admired the book and there could be no more ironic disciple. The Italian dictator first worked as a primary teacher where he was incapable of controlling his pupils. Evidently, he was in desperate need of a self-help book to recuperate a damaged ego. Benito also wrote a discourse on *The Prince*.

In the end the text may have been revolutionary in its day breaking with conventions and frankly outlining terms for ruling and maintaining one's rule, but such a treatise would not surprise so much today. In part, that is naturally due to the fact that we have been marked by Machiavelli's work, whether we are aware of it or not; we are all aware of the 'end-justifies-the-means' argument handed down to us by Niccolò.

On the other hand such a work would not shock us in quite the same way as it has done in previous epochs, purely because we have a clearer acceptance of who we are. The religious reactionary of bygone times has diminished and the chance to debate more openly has been generously indulged.

Man is the vane animal more than it ever was a social one. He may be selfish, violent, evil even, but nothing outrages our sense of dignity more than when this is plainly declared. Hitler, who had his military uniforms designed by Hugo Boss, would have also been deeply offended at any charge of being monstrous. He was part of the Aryan race, after all, blond-haired and blue eyed as he was, the contrary of a Chaplin comical character.

Perhaps Machiavelli's most striking achievement though, is more literary than political and invisible to the modern eye and ear. Machiavelli did for Italy what Chaucer did for England and that was win academic honours for his vernacular. What is truly remarkable then about the *The Prince* is that it was written in Italian and not Latin, breaking with centuries of scholastic tradition and setting a precedent for learning in his country.

Machiavelli also has the dubious honour of having become a member of a select literary élite whose names have become commonplace adjectives and in so doing he has joined the ranks of Kafka and Freud. Machiavellian is *a corrupt or manipulative person who deceives others for political gain,* and lately we need look no further than the lies propagated about the Iraq war in order to persuade the public to support, or at least, not protest against, an intervention for geo-political and petro-dollar financial gain. The author's name became a synonym for political maneuvers marked by astuteness and dishonesty.

However, as we have seen, this assumption is now being challenged on the grounds that it does not take into account any of his works other than *The Prince*. In fact, *The Prince* is not a complete work but rather the first volume of a two-piece effort with *Discourses on Livy* being the 'second volume'. Machiavelli wrote, *'I say that a people is more prudent, more stable and of better judgement than a prince.'* In other words, citizens in aggregate are wiser than a prince because a republic is better for adapting to change based, as it is, upon the diversity of opinions and experiences. It would also stand the test of time with greater fortitude than decisions taken by individual.

On reading this latter work we can then see through the seemingly contradictory writing of Machiavelli and better gauge his declarations. This was an observation shared by Henry Kissinger, who also said of the polemic author that, *'Like many realists he thought reality was self evident and in fact reality is the hardest thing to assess.'* Machiavelli saw human nature as never being conducted by a superior motive, which is unrealistic and where his theory comes unstuck.

He was probably more a social scientist showing us how things worked rather than applauding such feats and in so doing he clarified the moral ambiguities in the exercising of power. When one's survival is threatened, the possibilities of choice decrease with each subsequent act employed to preserve it, and with it the margin closes between what is a moral and immoral course of action. So, there is a physics of politics governed by the law of unintended consequences and you cannot fix a problem until you have first researched how that anomaly came about. Past politics worked in a Machiavellian mode due to underhand methods that sought to wrest control from its ruler. Remove such power struggles and a prince need not resort to such methods. Of course Machiavelli referred to a prince and not a democratic republic, which is our modern reality. Only if such sure footed foundations were to be challenged by 'underhand' means, would the government have to retaliate and probably along the lines Machiavelli suggested. As Machiavelli himself wrote in *The Prince*, *'for a man who strives after goodness in all his acts is sure to come to ruin, since there are so many men who are not good.'*

In conclusion then, Machiavelli's book has been placed in the pantheon of human thought because it touched upon a core human experience, such as political thought, like no other book before or since. Such universal works hold different messages at different times throughout history, such as Plato's *Republic* or works by Locke and Rousseau. In Machiavelli's final analysis he concluded that political decisions should be divorced from ethical matters, but not all. The decision as to which ethical issues could be ignored depended on the astute Prince best judging the political climate and more importantly, *fortuna*.

His motivation for the book was clearly stated in the pre-penultimate chapter, where he admitted it was a book for new princes who wished to appear as old princes, in spirit a cheat's guide for young nobles on the make who didn't want to become unhorsed.

The Prince was produced at a juncture in Europe's cultural development. It was the Renaissance, the April of Western Civilisation and the medieval era was ending. In its place arose the idea that man was master of his own fate. This led to the model of government as a human, not godly, creation and this groundbreaking change in perception was undoubtedly one of the era's greatest advances.

What was fundamentally rejected by readers was Machiavelli's belief that, *'The good Prince is not essentially the good man.'* This was something people did not wish to accept. However, there was method to his apparent madness as he explained that, *'I would rather teach them the way to hell so that they can go round it.' The Prince* then in its final reading is a guide book on how best to avoid unsound despotic rule.

The Prince, as we have seen, should be read in conjunction with Machiavelli's *The Discourses*. It was where he put his observations, previously delineated in *The Prince*, into a constitutional form. Therefore *The Discourses*, effectively the concluding part of his bi-political studies, ended with a Republic and not a dictatorship as the ideal form of governing not just a people but a nation. And it was the nation that most interested Machiavelli.

Today we have no autocratic princes governing princedoms but in Niccolò's time they were an integral part of the political scenery. Machiavelli was searching for work and killed two birds with the same book. He hoped to obtain employment and at the same time he threw himself headlong into the task of aiding stable government for Italy, something he had never known in his lifetime. We can't blame, what was an otherwise upstanding citizen in real life, for spelling out what we feared was true but preferred to be shielded from. Machiavelli was a patriot who sought the unification of his land and called upon Princes and the people to work towards that goal. Now with Republican and democratic governments the norm, it could therefore be concluded that Western Civilisation has become thoroughly Machiavellian in the author's own literary image. With that in mind, now try and condemn the man's writings.

'I commend myself to you. Be happy.'
Niccolò Machiavelli,
10 December, 1513

Mark Colenutt, editor of **Gilgamesh Books©**

IL PRINCIPE
DI NICOLO MACHIAVELLI
AL MAGNIFICO LORENZO
DI PIERO DE MEDICI.

LA VITA
DI CASTRVCCIO CASTRACANI
DA LVCCA.

IL MODO CHE TENNE
IL DVCA VALENTINO
PER AMMAZZARE VITELLOZZO VITELLI,
OLIVEROTTO DA FERMO, IL SIGNOR PAGOLO,
ET IL DVCA DI GRAVINA.

I RITRATTI
DELLE COSE DELLA FRANCIA,
ET DELL'ALAMAGNA.

M. D. L.

CONTENTS

by

MK Marriott (1908)

Translator of The Prince

The seal of the Magistrates
of the Ten of Liberty and Peace of the City of Florence
(c. early 1500s)

INTRODUCTION

Niccolò Machiavelli was born at Florence on 3rd May 1469. He was the second son of Bernardo di Niccolò Machiavelli, a lawyer of some repute, and of Bartolommea di Stefano Nelli, his wife. Both parents were members of the old Florentine nobility.

His life falls naturally into three periods, each of which singularly enough constitutes a distinct and important era in the history of Florence. His youth was concurrent with the greatness of Florence as an Italian power under the guidance of Lorenzo de' Medici, Il Magnifico. The downfall of the Medici in Florence occurred in 1494, in which year Machiavelli entered the public service. During his official career Florence was free under the government of a Republic, which lasted until 1512, when the Medici returned to power, and Machiavelli lost his office. The Medici again ruled Florence from 1512 until 1527, when they were once more driven out. This was the period of Machiavelli's literary activity and increasing influence; but he died, within a few weeks of the expulsion of the Medici, on 22nd June 1527, in his fifty-eighth year, without having regained office.

YOUTH — Aet. 1-25—1469-94

Although there is little recorded of the youth of Machiavelli, the Florence of those days is so well known that the early environment of this representative citizen may be easily imagined. Florence has been described as a city with two opposite currents of life, one directed by the fervent and austere Savonarola, the other by the splendour-loving Lorenzo. Savonarola's influence upon the young Machiavelli must have been slight, for although at one time he wielded immense power over the fortunes of Florence, he only furnished Machiavelli with a subject of a gibe in "The Prince," where he is cited as an example of an unarmed prophet who came to a bad end. Whereas the magnificence of the Medicean rule during the life of Lorenzo appeared to have impressed Machiavelli strongly, for he frequently recurs to it in his writings, and it is to Lorenzo's grandson that he dedicates "The Prince."

Machiavelli, in his "History of Florence," gives us a picture of the young men among whom his youth was passed. He writes: "They were freer than their forefathers in dress and living, and spent more in other kinds of excesses, consuming their time and money in idleness, gaming, and women; their chief aim was to appear well dressed and to speak with wit and acuteness, whilst he who could wound others the most cleverly was thought the wisest." In a letter to his son Guido, Machiavelli shows why youth should avail itself of its opportunities for study, and leads us to infer that his own youth had been so occupied. He writes: "I have received your letter, which has given me the greatest pleasure, especially because you tell me you are quite restored in health, than which I could have no better news; for if God grant life to you, and to me, I hope to make a good man of you if you are willing to do your share." Then, writing of a new patron, he continues: "This will turn out well for you, but it is necessary for you to study; since, then, you have no longer the excuse of illness, take pains to study letters and music, for you see what honour is done to me for the little skill I have. Therefore, my son, if you wish to please me, and to bring success and honour to yourself, do right and study, because others will help you if you help yourself."

OFFICE — Aet. 25-43—1494-1512

The second period of Machiavelli's life was spent in the service of the free Republic of Florence, which flourished, as stated above, from the expulsion of the Medici in 1494 until their return in 1512. After serving four years in one of the public offices he was appointed Chancellor and Secretary to the Second Chancery, the Ten of Liberty and Peace. Here we are on firm ground when dealing with the events of Machiavelli's life, for during this time he took a leading part in the affairs of the Republic, and we have its decrees, records, and dispatches to guide us, as well as his own writings. A mere recapitulation of a few of his transactions with the statesmen and soldiers of his time gives a fair indication of his activities, and supplies the sources from which he drew the experiences and characters which illustrate "The Prince."

His first mission was in 1499 to Catherina Sforza, "my lady of Forli" of "The Prince," from whose conduct and fate he drew the moral that it is far better to earn the confidence of the people than to rely on fortresses.

This is a very noticeable principle in Machiavelli, and is urged by him in many ways as a matter of vital importance to princes.

In 1500 he was sent to France to obtain terms from Louis XII for continuing the war against Pisa: this king it was who, in his conduct of affairs in Italy, committed the five capital errors in statecraft summarized in "The Prince," and was consequently driven out. He, also, it was who made the dissolution of his marriage a condition of support to Pope Alexander VI; which leads Machiavelli to refer those who urge that such promises should be kept to what he has written concerning the faith of princes.

Machiavelli's public life was largely occupied with events arising out of the ambitions of Pope Alexander VI and his son, Cesare Borgia, the Duke Valentino, and these characters fill a large space of "The Prince." Machiavelli never hesitates to cite the actions of the duke for the benefit of usurpers who wish to keep the states they have seized; he can, indeed, find no precepts to offer so good as the pattern of Cesare Borgia's conduct, insomuch that Cesare is acclaimed by some critics as the "hero" of "The Prince." Yet in "The Prince" the duke is in point of fact cited as a type of the man who rises on the fortune of others, and falls with them; who takes every course that might be expected from a prudent man but the course which will save him; who is prepared for all eventualities but the one which happens; and who, when all his abilities fail to carry him through, exclaims that it was not his fault, but an extraordinary and unforeseen fatality.

On the death of Pius III, in 1503, Machiavelli was sent to Rome to watch the election of his successor, and there he saw Cesare Borgia cheated into allowing the choice of the College to fall on Giuliano delle Rovere (Julius II), who was one of the cardinals that had most reason to fear the duke. Machiavelli, when commenting on this election, says that he who thinks new favours will cause great personages to forget old injuries deceives himself. Julius did not rest until he had ruined Cesare.

It was to Julius II that Machiavelli was sent in 1506, when that pontiff was commencing his enterprise against Bologna; which he brought to a successful issue, as he did many of his other adventures, owing chiefly to his impetuous character. It is in reference to Pope Julius that Machiavelli moralizes on the resemblance between Fortune and women, and concludes that it is the bold rather than the cautious man that will win and hold them both.

It is impossible to follow here the varying fortunes of the Italian states, which in 1507 were controlled by France, Spain, and Germany, with results that have lasted to our day; we are concerned with those events, and with the three great actors in them, so far only as they impinge on the personality of Machiavelli. He had several meetings with Louis XII of France, and his estimate of that monarch's character has already been alluded to. Machiavelli has painted Ferdinand of Aragon as the man who accomplished great things under the cloak of religion, but who in reality had no mercy, faith, humanity, or integrity; and who, had he allowed himself to be influenced by such motives, would have been ruined. The Emperor Maximilian was one of the most interesting men of the age, and his character has been drawn by many hands; but Machiavelli, who was an envoy at his court in 1507-8, reveals the secret of his many failures when he describes him as a secretive man, without force of character—ignoring the human agencies necessary to carry his schemes into effect, and never insisting on the fulfilment of his wishes.

The remaining years of Machiavelli's official career were filled with events arising out of the League of Cambrai, made in 1508 between the three great European powers already mentioned and the pope, with the object of crushing the Venetian Republic. This result was attained in the battle of Vaila, when Venice lost in one day all that she had won in eight hundred years. Florence had a difficult part to play during these events, complicated as they were by the feud which broke out between the pope and the French, because friendship with France had dictated the entire policy of the Republic. When, in 1511, Julius II finally formed the Holy League against France, and with the assistance of the Swiss drove the French out of Italy, Florence lay at the mercy of the Pope, and had to submit to his terms, one of which was that the Medici should be restored. The return of the Medici to Florence on 1st September 1512, and the consequent fall of the Republic, was the signal for the dismissal of Machiavelli and his friends, and thus put an end to his public career, for, as we have seen, he died without regaining office.

LITERATURE AND DEATH — Aet. 43-58—1512-27

On the return of the Medici, Machiavelli, who for a few weeks had vainly hoped to retain his office under the new masters of Florence, was dismissed by decree dated 7th November 1512. Shortly after this he was accused of complicity in an abortive conspiracy against the Medici, imprisoned, and put to the question by torture. The new Medicean pope, Leo X, procured his release, and he retired to his small property at San Casciano, near Florence, where he devoted himself to literature. In a letter to Francesco Vettori, dated 13th December 1513, he has left a very interesting description of his life at this period, which elucidates his methods and his motives in writing "The Prince." After describing his daily occupations with his family and neighbours, he writes: "The evening being come, I return home and go to my study; at the entrance I pull off my peasant-clothes, covered with dust and dirt, and put on my noble court dress, and thus becomingly re-clothed I pass into the ancient courts of the men of old, where, being lovingly received by them, I am fed with that food which is mine alone; where I do not hesitate to speak with them, and to ask for the reason of their actions, and they in their benignity answer me; and for four hours I feel no weariness, I forget every trouble, poverty does not dismay, death does not terrify me; I am possessed entirely by those great men. And because Dante says:

Knowledge doth come of learning well retained,
Unfruitful else,

I have noted down what I have gained from their conversation, and have composed a small work on 'Principalities,' where I pour myself out as fully as I can in meditation on the subject, discussing what a principality is, what kinds there are, how they can be acquired, how they can be kept, why they are lost: and if any of my fancies ever pleased you, this ought not to displease you: and to a prince, especially to a new one, it should be welcome: therefore I dedicate it to his Magnificence Giuliano. Filippo Casavecchio has seen it; he will be able to tell you what is in it, and of the discourses I have had with him; nevertheless, I am still enriching and polishing it."

The "little book" suffered many vicissitudes before attaining the form in which it has reached us. Various mental influences were at work during its composition; its title and patron were changed; and for some unknown reason it was finally dedicated to Lorenzo de' Medici. Although Machiavelli discussed with Casavecchio whether it should be sent or presented in person to the patron, there is no evidence that Lorenzo ever received or even read it: he certainly never gave Machiavelli any employment. Although it was plagiarized during Machiavelli's lifetime, "The Prince" was never published by him, and its text is still disputable.

Machiavelli concludes his letter to Vettori thus: "And as to this little thing [his book], when it has been read it will be seen that during the fifteen years I have given to the study of statecraft I have neither slept nor idled; and men ought ever to desire to be served by one who has reaped experience at the expense of others. And of my loyalty none could doubt, because having always kept faith I could not now learn how to break it; for he who has been faithful and honest, as I have, cannot change his nature; and my poverty is a witness to my honesty."

Before Machiavelli had got "The Prince" off his hands he commenced his "Discourse on the First Decade of Titus Livius," which should be read concurrently with "The Prince." These and several minor works occupied him until the year 1518, when he accepted a small commission to look after the affairs of some Florentine merchants at Genoa. In 1519 the Medicean rulers of Florence granted a few political concessions to her citizens, and Machiavelli with others was consulted upon a new constitution under which the Great Council was to be restored; but on one pretext or another it was not promulgated.

In 1520 the Florentine merchants again had recourse to Machiavelli to settle their difficulties with Lucca, but this year was chiefly remarkable for his re-entry into Florentine literary society, where he was much sought after, and also for the production of his "Art of War." It was in the same year that he received a commission at the instance of Cardinal de' Medici to write the "History of Florence," a task which occupied him until 1525. His return to popular favour may have determined the Medici to give him this employment, for an old writer observes that "an able statesman out of work, like a huge whale, will endeavour to overturn the ship unless he has an empty cask to play with."

When the "History of Florence" was finished, Machiavelli took it to Rome for presentation to his patron, Giuliano de' Medici, who had in the meanwhile become pope under the title of Clement VII. It is somewhat remarkable that, as, in 1513, Machiavelli had written "The Prince" for the instruction of the Medici after they had just regained power in Florence, so, in 1525, he dedicated the "History of Florence" to the head of the family when its ruin was now at hand. In that year the battle of Pavia destroyed the French rule in Italy, and left Francis I a prisoner in the hands of his great rival, Charles V. This was followed by the sack of Rome, upon the news of which the popular party at Florence threw off the yoke of the Medici, who were once more banished.

Machiavelli was absent from Florence at this time, but hastened his return, hoping to secure his former office of secretary to the "Ten of Liberty and Peace." Unhappily he was taken ill soon after he reached Florence, where he died on 22nd June 1527.

THE MAN AND HIS WORKS

No one can say where the bones of Machiavelli rest, but modern Florence has decreed him a stately cenotaph in Santa Croce, by the side of her most famous sons; recognizing that, whatever other nations may have found in his works, Italy found in them the idea of her unity and the germs of her renaissance among the nations of Europe. Whilst it is idle to protest against the world-wide and evil signification of his name, it may be pointed out that the harsh construction of his doctrine which this sinister reputation implies was unknown to his own day, and that the researches of recent times have enabled us to interpret him more reasonably. It is due to these inquiries that the shape of an "unholy necromancer," which so long haunted men's vision, has begun to fade.

Machiavelli was undoubtedly a man of great observation, acuteness, and industry; noting with appreciative eye whatever passed before him, and with his supreme literary gift turning it to account in his enforced retirement from affairs. He does not present himself, nor is he depicted by his contemporaries, as a type of that rare combination, the successful statesman and author, for he appears to have been only moderately prosperous in his several embassies and political employments. He was misled by Catherina Sforza, ignored by Louis XII, overawed by Cesare Borgia; several of his embassies were quite barren of results; his attempts to fortify Florence failed, and the soldiery that he raised astonished everybody by their cowardice. In the conduct of his own affairs he was timid and time-serving; he dared not appear by the side of Soderini, to whom he owed so much, for fear of compromising himself; his connection with the Medici was open to suspicion, and Giuliano appears to have recognized his real forte when he set him to write the "History of Florence," rather than employ him in the state. And it is on the literary side of his character, and there alone, that we find no weakness and no failure.

Although the light of almost four centuries has been focused on "The Prince," its problems are still debatable and interesting, because they are the eternal problems between the ruled and their rulers. Such as they are, its ethics are those of Machiavelli's contemporaries; yet they cannot be said to be out of date so long as the governments of Europe rely on material rather than on moral forces. Its historical incidents and personages become interesting by reason of the uses which Machiavelli makes of them to illustrate his theories of government and conduct.

Leaving out of consideration those maxims of state which still furnish some European and eastern statesmen with principles of action, "The Prince" is bestrewn with truths that can be proved at every turn. Men are still the dupes of their simplicity and greed, as they were in the days of Alexander VI. The cloak of religion still conceals the vices which Machiavelli laid bare in the character of Ferdinand of Aragon. Men will not look at things as they really are, but as they wish them to be—and are ruined. In politics there are no perfectly safe courses; prudence consists in choosing the least dangerous ones. Then—to pass to a higher plane—Machiavelli reiterates that, although crimes may win an empire, they do not win glory. Necessary wars are just wars, and the arms of a nation are hallowed when it has no other resource but to fight.

It is the cry of a far later day than Machiavelli's that government should be elevated into a living moral force, capable of inspiring the people with a just recognition of the fundamental principles of society; to this "high argument" "The Prince" contributes but little. Machiavelli always refused to write either of men or of governments otherwise than as he found them, and he writes with such skill and insight that his work is of abiding value. But what invests "The Prince" with more than a merely artistic or historical interest is the incontrovertible truth that it deals with the great principles which still guide nations and rulers in their relationship with each other and their neighbours.

In translating "The Prince" my aim has been to achieve at all costs an exact literal rendering of the original, rather than a fluent paraphrase adapted to the modern notions of style and expression. Machiavelli was no facile phrasemonger; the conditions under which he wrote obliged him to weigh every word; his themes were lofty, his substance grave, his manner nobly plain and serious. "Quis eo fuit unquam in partiundis rebus, in definiendis, in explanandis pressior?" In "The Prince," it may be truly said, there is reason assignable, not only for every word, but for the position of every word. To an Englishman of Shakespeare's time the translation of such a treatise was in some ways a comparatively easy task, for in those times the genius of the English more nearly resembled that of the Italian language; to the Englishman of to-day it is not so simple. To take a single example: the word "intrattenere," employed by Machiavelli to indicate the policy adopted by the Roman Senate towards the weaker states of Greece, would by an Elizabethan be correctly rendered "entertain," and every contemporary reader would understand what was meant by saying that "Rome entertained the Aetolians and the Achaeans without augmenting their power." But to-day such a phrase would seem obsolete and ambiguous, if not unmeaning: we are compelled to say that "Rome maintained friendly relations with the Aetolians," etc., using four words to do the work of one. I have tried to preserve the pithy brevity of the Italian so far as was consistent with an absolute fidelity to the sense. If the result be an occasional asperity I can only hope that the reader, in his eagerness to reach the author's meaning, may overlook the roughness of the road that leads him to it.

The following is a list of the works of Machiavelli:

Principal works. Discorso sopra le cose di Pisa, 1499; Del modo di trattare i popoli della Valdichiana ribellati, 1502; Del modo tenuto dal duca Valentino nell' ammazzare Vitellozzo Vitelli, Oliverotto da Fermo, etc., 1502; Discorso sopra la provisione del danaro, 1502; Decennale primo (poem in terza rima), 1506; Ritratti delle cose dell' Alemagna, 1508-12; Decennale secondo, 1509; Ritratti delle cose di Francia, 1510; Discorsi sopra la prima deca di T. Livio, 3 vols., 1512-17; Il Principe, 1513; Andria, comedy translated from Terence, 1513 (?); Mandragola, prose comedy in five acts, with prologue in verse, 1513; Della lingua (dialogue), 1514; Clizia, comedy in prose, 1515 (?); Belfagor arcidiavolo (novel), 1515; Asino d'oro (poem in terza rima), 1517; Dell' arte della guerra, 1519-20; Discorso sopra il riformare lo stato di Firenze, 1520; Sommario delle cose della citta di Lucca, 1520; Vita di Castruccio Castracani da Lucca, 1520; Istorie fiorentine, 8 books, 1521-5; Frammenti storici, 1525.

Other poems include Sonetti, Canzoni, Ottave, and Canti carnascialeschi.

Editions. Aldo, Venice, 1546; della Tertina, 1550; Cambiagi, Florence, 6 vols., 1782-5; dei Classici, Milan, 10 1813; Silvestri, 9 vols., 1820-2; Passerini, Fanfani, Milanesi, 6 vols. only published, 1873-7.

Minor works. Ed. F. L. Polidori, 1852; Lettere familiari, ed. E. Alvisi, 1883, 2 editions, one with excisions; Credited Writings, ed. G. Canestrini, 1857; Letters to F. Vettori, see A. Ridolfi, Pensieri intorno allo scopo di N. Machiavelli nel libro Il Principe, etc.; D. Ferrara, The Private Correspondence of Nicolo Machiavelli, 1929.

DEDICATION

To the Magnificent Lorenzo Di Piero De' Medici:

Those who strive to obtain the good graces of a prince are accustomed to come before him with such things as they hold most precious, or in which they see him take most delight; whence one often sees horses, arms, cloth of gold, precious stones, and similar ornaments presented to princes, worthy of their greatness.

Desiring therefore to present myself to your Magnificence with some testimony of my devotion towards you, I have not found among my possessions anything which I hold more dear than, or value so much as, the knowledge of the actions of great men, acquired by long experience in contemporary affairs, and a continual study of antiquity; which, having reflected upon it with great and prolonged diligence, I now send, digested into a little volume, to your Magnificence.

And although I may consider this work unworthy of your countenance, nevertheless I trust much to your benignity that it may be acceptable, seeing that it is not possible for me to make a better gift than to offer you the opportunity of understanding in the shortest time all that I have learnt in so many years, and with so many troubles and dangers; which work I have not embellished with swelling or magnificent words, nor stuffed with rounded periods, nor with any extrinsic allurements or adornments whatever, with which so many are accustomed to embellish their works; for I have wished either that no honour should be given it, or else that the truth of the matter and the weightiness of the theme shall make it acceptable.

Nor do I hold with those who regard it as a presumption if a man of low and humble condition dare to discuss and settle the concerns of princes; because, just as those who draw landscapes place themselves below in the plain to contemplate the nature of the mountains and of lofty places, and in order to contemplate the plains place themselves upon high mountains, even so to understand the nature of the people it needs to be a prince, and to understand that if princes it needs to be of the people.

Take then, your Magnificence, this little gift in the spirit in which I send it; wherein, if it be diligently read and considered by you, you will learn my extreme desire that you should attain that greatness which fortune and your other attributes promise. And if your Magnificence from the summit of your greatness will sometimes turn your eyes to these lower regions, you will see how unmeritedly I suffer a great and continued malignity of fortune.

HANDBOOK
to the Legacy & Odyssey of
Don QuiXote

- Everything the armchair academic needs to know about the greatest novel ever written –

Don Quixote is considered by the literally great and good to be the best novel ever written. It holds the record for the most translations, relegating even the Bible to second best. It is considered the first modern novel and there are those that commit themselves to read it every year. So what is it this book contains in its ageing pages that makes it so exceptional and has provoked such an earnest reaction for over four centuries?

This unique handbook, therefore, is for the culturally curious, for those who wish to grapple with the greater picture of world literature and its universal meaning. If Don Quixote is on your 'Bucket List' but you are not sure you have the time to cross it off by reading the whole tome, then this is the book for you.

This illustrated publication will save you the trek through Spain's badlands and provide you with a broad image of the man, the novel and its principal characters before delving into the wider philosophical message that it safeguards for all humanity. Despite this, if you are still keen to make the trip to Spain in person, then this volume ends with a personal tour of the captivating Quixote Route of La Mancha.

By the time you come to turn the last page your reading will only urge you to pick up the original manuscript and release your imagination upon the barren plains of late medieval Spain. Once you find yourself confronted by Cervantes' superlatively famous first line, you will have been profoundly prepared before you venture off into Cervantes' masterpiece and head for the windmills on the horizon of Castile.

5056862R00034

Printed in Great Britain
by Amazon.co.uk, Ltd.,
Marston Gate.